AN INTRODUCTION TO

BUDDHISM

Compiled and edited by
Diana St.Ruth

BUDDHIST PUBLISHING GROUP

Buddhist Publishing Group
Sharpham North
Ashprington
Totnes
Devon
TQ9 7UT
England

British Library Cataloguing
in Publication Data

An introduction to Buddhism. — 2nd ed.
  1. Buddhism
  I. St.Ruth, Diana
  294.3

  ISBN 0-946672-22-9

Printed and bound in Great Britain
by Billings & Sons Limited, Worcester

In memory of
ROSA TAYLOR

CONTENTS

Abbreviations

Chin.	Chinese
Jap.	Japanese
P.	Pali
Skt.	Sanskrit
Tib.	Tibetan
Lit.	Literally

LIST OF ILLUSTRATIONS

Illustrations on pages 10, 21, 25 and 52 by Marcelle Hanselaar.

INTRODUCTION

The Buddha's teaching was given in order to help people understand their true nature, their Buddha-nature, so that they may be released from suffering.

In order to know about Buddhism, therefore, we have to know about ourselves. We have to be aware of our actions, beliefs, views and opinions; we have to be aware of what we mean when using such words as 'I', 'me', or 'mine'. This process of understanding is called treading the Buddhist Path.

You yourself must make the effort.
Buddhas only point the way.
Those who have entered the Path
and who meditate
will be freed from the fetters of illusion.

The Dhammapada, v.276

THE BUDDHA

Siddhartha Gautama, born approximately two thousand six hundred years ago, was the man who became the Buddha, the Fully Enlightened One. The legends surrounding the life of Siddhartha are varied, but they have a common theme. He was born of a  royal family of the Sakya clan in Kapilavastu on the borders of Nepal and India. His early life was one of luxury and ease, later enhanced by his marriage to Yasodhara and the birth of his son, Rahula. But at the age of twenty-nine his life underwent a dramatic change.

Siddhartha became deeply aware as if for the very first time, that all beings were subject to aging, sickness and death; he saw the truth of change and the impermanence of all things. This realization hit him with such force that his luxurious way of life completely lost its charm. He suddenly wanted to know the reasons for life's woe — why people suffered in poverty and sickness; why all beings were born, apparently just to die.

Despite the pleas of Yasodhara (his wife) and King Suddhodhana (his father), Siddhartha left home in search of truth and enlightenment. He lived as did other holy men of India in those days, wearing rags and begging food, or surviving on the fruits of the forest, and sometimes not eating at all. He learned how to be an ascetic, how to meditate, and how to perform rites and rituals.

Six years went by, six austere years of searching, which left him weak and near to death. Then one day he realized the futility of his actions; he realized that religious rites and rituals, the adoption of philosophical views and the self-infliction of pain by practising austerities did not lead to truth. He suddenly understood that to kill the senses was as bad as overindulging the senses, both being ambitious vain pursuits, while the questions of his heart and mind remained unanswered. Was there release from suffering; was there release from birth, decay and death?

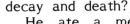

He ate a meal of rice. Strong again, revitalized and inspired, he sought the cool of a tree. Now he was ready. Touching the earth with his hand, he called upon it to bear witness, saying he would not rise from that spot until complete enlightenment had been realized.

Siddhartha's mind grown tired of beliefs, views and opinions, became tranquil, yet alert. He observed the nature of existence, the nature of desire; he observed that dissatisfaction and suffering arose when desire arose. He experienced the total cessation of desire and realized that this was the cessation of all suffering.

Then came the realization that because mind and body are impermanent, they are not self. This led to the understanding that it was attachment to mind and body which gave rise to the idea of self, which in turn gave rise to the idea of birth, decay and death. The truth of nonbirth, nondecay, nondeath were then realized and all manner of mysteries unfolded before him — he became the Fully Awakened One, Buddha.

For the following forty-five years Siddhartha Gautama, the Buddha, taught devotees and disciples of all kinds — men and women, rich and poor, young and old, of any caste or creed. And this is the essence of what he taught:

To be aware, as awareness is the central core of right living and the door to enlightenment.

To live in a moral way, as immorality destroys awareness and causes suffering.

To refrain from harming any living being, as no being likes to suffer.

To refrain from all attachment, as non-attachment is freedom from suffering.

To choose to be wise and to abandon ignorance, as ignorance is at the heart of all suffering.

To be selfless, as selfishness is painful and causes ignorance.

To be patient, because all things are impermanent.

To be compassionate and to seek liberation for the benefit of all beings.

To wake up to the illusion of time and space, and to understand that all ideas and beliefs are empty.

The historical details relating to the life of the Buddha are debatable but not too important.   It is the teaching itself that matters.   And the teaching, which is based upon the realization of truth, has to be seen by each person for himself; no one else can see it for him.   Buddhas merely point the way.

Siddhartha Gautama,
Born a long time ago,
Died a long time ago.
Buddha — never born, never died.

REBIRTH

There are those who believe that birth only occurs once — one birth which will lead to one death. Such people are called nihilists; they believe in annihilation. There are others who believe that each of us has been born time and time again and will die time and time again, or that we shall continue after death in some kind of heaven or hell state. These people are called eternalists; they believe in eternity.

The Buddha held neither view. Why? Because he saw truth and did not have to conceptualize about it. The Buddha's realization of truth led him to understand just how foolish it was to attach oneself to views which falsely interpret life and only serve to block experience.

Annihilation is a view. Eternity is a view. The truth has nothing to do with either.

Annihilation is not an
alternative to eternity,
It's just an alternative concept.

The Buddha remembered former lives, not one or two, but hundreds. He gave the analogy of a man going from village to village. 'The man,' he said, 'may afterwards consider, "I went from my own village to another village where I stood, sat and spoke in such a manner. Then I went to another village and stood, sat and spoke in another manner."' This is how the Buddha described the way one might remember various former habitations or lives.* These recollections, however, did not lead the Buddha to adopting an eternalistic view.

Experiences themselves change. The essence of what we are to ourselves, however, does not change. 'There is an unborn, an unaging, an undying,' said the Buddha. And Hui Neng, the Sixth Chinese Ch'an/Zen Patriarch expressed his realization of the unborn in this way, 'Who would have thought that the essence of mind is intrinsically free from becoming or annihilation! Who would have thought that the essence of mind is intrinsically free from change!'**

When we are aware and unattached to conditions, we shall see that the essence of our being does not alter, that it is only circumstances and conditions that alter. All things in life change. Seeing this constant change is the way to become aware of the

* See 'Greater Discourse at Assapura', I.B. Horner (trans.), The Middle Length Sayings, Vol. I.
** Wong Mou-Lam (trans.), The Sutra of Hui Neng.

unchanging. The body grows old, day becomes night, spring becomes summer, satisfaction becomes dissatisfaction, sadness becomes happiness, birth becomes death, and so on. all things are impermanent. If we are aware, we shall see that there is nothing permanent or static which moves through life or through time; we shall realize that one thing is experienced and then something else is experienced. It is almost as if this moment were the only permanently static thing, in which all other things manifested. But this is just another description and should therefore not be grasped as the truth.

Each experience is completely new and fresh. No part of it has been dragged from the past and no part will be carried into the future.

Childhood, youth, and old age, are experienced and when the body is dying, dying will be experienced. We to ourselves, the essence of what we are, however, is none of these things. The essence of what we are is unborn, undying; it is deathless and beyond change.

Just see the freedom in impermanence.

We may believe ourselves to be living in a body, at a particular point in time. This is the illusion of birth. The Buddha was able to recognize this illusion — first in himself and then in others. He taught that we should not look upon body and mind as self. If we think we are the body or the mind, this only causes suffering.

Because of attachment to mind and body, we are born and reborn in delusion. When there is the slightest attachment to the six senses,* concepts about birth and death, eternity and annihilation are inevitable. Attachment to the senses is the striving to gain pleasure and enjoyment for the senses. Birth or rebirth is the illusion which occurs when we crave the satisfaction of the senses. When we do not crave the pleasures of the senses, when we do not have attachment to mind and body, then we come away from the illusion of a self living in the body — being born, growing old and dying. Then the illusion of birth ceases.

To be free of the illusion of a being is to be free of the illusion of birth.

But these [physical, mental and formless selves] are only designations, figures of speech, expressions, concepts, belonging to the world, and the Tathagata makes use of them without being bound to, or holding on to, any of them.

The Buddha
Potthapada Sutta, Long Discourses of the Buddha
A.A.G. Bennett (trans.)

---

* Sight, sound, smell, taste, touch and the thinking mind. In Buddhism mind is regarded as a sense, along with the other five.

*There are no beings, Subhuti, nor are there
not any beings. The Tathagata says all
beings are not beings; they are just called
beings.*

The Buddha
The Diamond Sutra

The Buddha spoke of beings caught up in
illusion. He spoke of rebirth into good conditions and into bad conditions. He said that
it was possible to observe beings passing
away or coming to be, to comprehend that
beings were mean, good, attractive, ugly,
and so forth as a result of their previous
deeds. He said it was possible to know that
these beings who did unwholesome deeds of
body, speech and mind, at the breaking up of
the body after dying have arisen in a sor-
rowful state, but those beings who did
wholesome deeds of body, speech and mind,
at the breaking up of the body after dying
have arisen in a good state. He gave the
analogy of a man standing between two
houses, seeing people going back and forth,
and he said that in this way it is possible to
see beings passing away and coming to be
into good or bad states.*
The Buddha, however, encouraged people
to see the unsatisfactoriness of all conditions. He taught that when the self-
centred activity of craving, grasping and

* See 'Greater Discourse at Assapura', I.B. Horner
(trans.), The Middle Length Sayings, Vol. I.

clinging stops, then the sense of self stops and rebirth stops. And he taught that this is *not* annihilation but merely the cessation of delusion.

The only 'self' anyone really has is Buddha, the unborn, the undying. Unfortunately, we defile this Buddha-nature life after life and suffer as a result.

> *We are all contemporaries of*
> *beginningless time,*
> *Yet we run in fear of death.*

When we are aware and unattached, we shall experience in this very moment total freedom from mind and body. In Buddhism this experience may be referred to as Nirvana, or Nirodha, Buddha-nature, Dharma-kaya, Enlightenment, Tathagata, Buddha, Suchness, Essence of Mind, Birthlessness, Deathlessness, Anatta, Void, or Reality — it has many names but the experience is the same.

Trying to understand rebirth intellectually is very difficult. We are attached to notions about ourselves and other people, and when we are told that mind and body are not self, it can be very confusing. This is the reason Buddhism discourages intellectual speculation and encourages direct experience. Truth is ever present. If we want to be aware of truth for ourselves, we should really attend to what is taking place in this moment, and then we shall see the folly of eternalism and the impossibility of annihilation.

KARMA

Karma means action, and karma-vipaka means the ripening of actions. Usually in the West this process of action and reaction is all simply referred to as karma.

Actions are like invisible seeds planted in the unborn. If the seed is bad the fruit will be bad, and if the seed is good, the fruit will also be good. Every action of body, speech and mind, no matter how small, is subject to this natural law.

If we steal something, for example, we sow a bad seed. Feelings of guilt, fear of detection, general discomfort and irritation will inevitably arise. These are immediate reactions. Deception and lies, detection, reprimand and general unhappiness may be the more far-reaching reactions.

If we speak harshly or unkindly to someone, the immediate reactions are likely to be harsh words in return, argument, ill feeling or a guilty conscience. The far-reaching reactions may be enmity and slander.

If we wish harm for others or are secretly pleased at their misfortune, if we are irritated by situations and wish they were different, mental conflict will be the immediate reaction. Worry, general unhappiness and mental illness may be the far-reaching reactions.

Karma is not an outside force. We sow and reap in the field of causation (our

natural daily lives). No one else is responsible for the way we act and no one else is
responsible for our karma.

All emotional states are karmic. If we
feel good it is because we have done something good in body, speech, or mind. If we
feel ill at ease, it is because we have done
something which has brought about that condition. It is a very simple law of cause and
effect.

> *'Cease to do evil, learn to*
> *do good, purify your heart.'*
> *This is the teaching of all the Buddhas.*
>
> The Dhammapada, v. 183

We may wonder about the many innocent
people who live in unfortunate circumstances
and compare them to the many who have an
abundance of good fortune. We may wonder
whether there is really any justice in the
world. But if we look beyond the superficial,
we shall see the real. Some people are rich
and healthy and enjoy their good fortune.
Others are rich and healthy but suffer —
they suffer inwardly. Some people are
impoverished and sick and suffer terribly,
while others are impoverished and sick but
have peace in their hearts and minds. Not
everyone reacts in the same way to similar
conditions.

We should not assume that a rich or
healthy person has good karma while a poor
or unhealthy one has bad. We cannot know

the type of karma people have by their material possessions or physical wellbeing. Whether a person is at peace or not depends upon his inner attitude toward the world, not upon outer circumstances.

Adverse conditions are great teachers. To those seeking truth and enlightenment, they should be accepted as such. They teach tolerance, patience and kindness, from which wisdom and compassion spring forth. That which appears to be bad karma from a worldly point of view, may in fact be good karma from a spiritual point of view, and vice versa.

Not one single action is beyond the reach of karma. When even the tiniest pebble is dropped into a pond, ripples still form, travel to the outer banks and then return. If we pay attention to what happens to us in our daily lives, we shall

Kwan-yin

become aware of this law at work. We may not like the idea of karma, nor want to believe it. It may be disturbing to think that, from moment to moment, we are in the conditions most suitable for us.

We may desperately want to acquire something or be rid of something in our lives. But if we try to attain anything for which we are not karmically entitled, if the time is not right, then we shall not succeed. The very thing for which we yearn and crave will elude us, no matter what we do. In the same way, any conditions from which we try to escape will recreate themselves wherever we go until their time is over.

With only an intellectual understanding of karma, we may adopt a cold-hearted attitude towards life. When we see others suffering or in bad circumstances, we may foolishly say, 'Oh, that is their karma; they must have done something terrible to deserve it.' To judge others in this way will also have its karmic effect on us. To judge others is to be at fault ourselves. When we see others suffering it is our karma to see it, and it may be our karma to help. With wisdom we shall know what to do. In any case, it is never our right to judge others.

Nor, with regard to ourselves, should we be pessimistic and say, 'Oh well, there's nothing I can do about it; it's my karma.' On the contrary, it is precisely because it *is* our karma that we *can* do something about it.

BEYOND KARMA

In a certain sense there is no such thing as good karma. Truly 'good' karma is no karma. If we think good thoughts, do good deeds, say good things with the intention of receiving good results, then our motives are entirely self-centred. We may receive good results. We may also receive feelings of self-satisfaction, self-righteousness, superiority and conceit. Thinking of oneself as a 'good' person who does 'good' things is a way of thinking which cannot lead to enlightenment or Nirvana; it is not the Buddhist way.

Those who tread the Buddhist path will see good and bad karma as two sides of the same coin. They will then learn how to transcend both good and bad karma. The Buddha taught that one should do what is right without regard for oneself; then there will be no karma. This is supremely good; it is Nirvana.

When karma is transcended, when we are free from pleasure, pain, praise and blame, then there is liberation and enlightenment. Understanding truth when it is spoken of is the experience of enlightenment. This experience is beyond karma. Being wise, compassionate and tolerant is beyond karma. Becoming aware of deathlessness and the Buddha-nature within us is beyond karma.

Delusion is karmic.
What are you doing now
that keeps you in ignorance?

Enlightenment is spontaneous.
What are you doing now
that keeps you in ignorance?

When Bodhidharma (the first Ch'an/Zen Patriarch) went to China and the Emperor asked him what merits to expect from building temples, permitting monks to be ordained, giving alms, etc., Bodhidharma replied that such deeds did not warrant any merit. The Emperor may have earned good karma, but he earned nothing for the heart and mind. When we are blameless in body, speech and mind, then we shall be free of karma.

Bodhidharma

MEDITATION

The purpose of Buddhist meditation is to see that mind and body are impermanent and not self, and that attachment to them is the cause of all suffering. To meditate is to live totally in the moment in a blameless, selfless way; it is to realize freedom from karma and rebirth.

AWARENESS

Meditation is a form of awareness. Many of us are not usually very aware in our lives. For most of the time we tend to think about the past and the future, and almost ignore the present.

If we wish to meditate, we should learn how to become fully aware of what is taking place in the moment.

When walking we should be really in the walking, taking every step with complete attention, feeling the movements and sensations of the body. The same with sitting, lying down, eating, hearing, seeing, smelling, tasting and touching — we should really *know* what is taking place in the present moment, paying attention to all physical actions and sensations as they occur.

We shall probably find that thoughts and daydreams interfere with our attempts at being aware. Such thoughts and daydreams should be dropped as soon as they arise.

As we become accustomed to being aware of the body, our area of awareness may be expanded to include the mind. All actions are preceded by intention: before we move, we have the intention to move; before we speak, we have the intention to speak, and so on. When we are very aware, we shall notice these intentions.

Next we should become aware of reactions. Many of our actions are not straightforward; they are reactions. It is as if we are programmed so that when key words or circumstances are fed into us, we come up with set responses. These are habit-patterns which have developed over the years. When we are aware, we shall see these tendencies. Seeing them will give us the opportunity of dropping them and thereby living in a more harmonious and spontaneous way.

Finally, we should include the observation of emotions in our awareness: anger, infatuation, hate, jealousy, fear, hope, disappointment . . . Emotions drain our energy, leaving us feeling exhausted, depressed and unhappy. When we see emotions as the cause of pain and suffering, then we cease to want to have anything to do with them. We can then abandon them. When our energies are not channelled into emotional states, they are channelled into heightened awareness, wisdom and compassion.

Awareness of the body will reveal to us that the body is not self. Likewise with the mind.   When we really investigate the mind, we shall realize that all mental activity is impermanent and, as such, is not self. Seeing that mind and body are not self, is liberation.

SITTING MEDITATION

In order to sit in formal meditation, one needs to adopt an upright posture (either sitting on a chair or cross-legged on the floor).   The hands may be rested, palms up, one upon the other in the lap, the eyes fully or half closed, and the mind directed towards a predetermined object of concentration — ideally the breathing process.   One of the following objects of concentration may be taken up:

(a) The breaths may be counted (not out loud, but in thought only) — breathe in, count 'one', breathe out, count 'one', breathe in, count 'two', breathe out, count 'two', and so on up to 'ten'.   After ten complete breaths have been counted, start again at 'one'.   If concentration is lost before ten breaths have been counted, then also start again at 'one'.

(b) Alternatively, the breath passing through the nostrils may be the object of concentration. As the breath is inhaled, the nostrils become cool; as it is exhaled they become warm. These cool and warm sensations may be the objects of concentration.

(c) Or the rise and fall of the abdomen may be the object of concentration. The point of observation for this is about three finger-widths below the navel. Here the gentle rise and fall of the abdomen should be observed as the breath is inhaled and exhaled.

The breathing process should *never* be altered. The purpose is to observe the breathing process, not to play around with it. This is very important to understand; otherwise we shall not be practising Buddhist meditation and may even get ourselves into trouble. Of course, the breathing process may alter naturally as we observe it. It may become very calm, almost imperceptible, but that is not the same as forcing oneself to breathe in a certain way.

The object of concentration (in this case the breathing process) is like an anchorage point for the mind. When the mind wanders, therefore, it should be brought back to the object of concentration. This bringing the mind back, may have to be undertaken time and time again in the early stages.

To meditate, in the Buddhist sense, is simply to be aware of what is actually taking place in the moment. While we are concentrating we are not indulging in any emotional state or mental conflict. As we become accustomed to watching the breath, we learn to appreciate those thought-free moments more and more.   Then, when the time is right, we may let go of any object of concentration and just sit, free of the constant play of thought and free of concentration too.   This is the highest form of meditation — being open and free of all discursive thought.   It should be understood that this is not a trance state or a condition of sleep.   On the contrary, it is an awakened state wherein we realize total freedom of mind.

We should sit, without moving, for a predetermined length of time; otherwise our minds will be occupied with thoughts about moving or finishing the meditation.   It is customary to sit for up to an hour or so at a time.   As the aim of Buddhist meditation is to see directly into the unborn, undying moment, the length of time involved in sitting is unimportant; it is the quality of the meditation that matters.

Sitting meditation is an incredibly valuable and worthwhile exercise.   However, it should never be allowed to degenerate into a mere habit, or we shall go through the motions of meditating without actually doing it.   We could also be *reinforcing* ideas of time and self — a self undergoing training for a period of time in order to reach a desired goal.   This would be the very reverse of what the Buddha intended.   Nevertheless it is an easy trap to fall into.

Essentially, meditation has nothing to do with the position of the body. We can do it anywhere and at any time. The essence of Buddhist meditation is awareness, honest investigation, looking directly at life and at ourselves, and seeing all things for what they are.

As we become accustomed to awareness, we shall cease to regard it as a practice; it will simply become our natural way of life.

Mindfulness is the path to the Deathless;
Negligence is the path to death.
The mindful do not die.
The negligent are already like the dead.
                                    The Dhammapada, v. 21

NONATTACHMENT

Pleasant sights catch the eye;
Awareness frees the heart.

Nonattachment is a result of awareness. If we see something pleasant and do not desire it, we are free from attachment. If we see something unpleasant and do not feel any aversion towards it, we are also free from attachment. When we get caught up in desire or aversion we are bound by those things, we are attached, and we suffer. We should avoid becoming attached to anything that arises in life.

If we only think about events instead of being aware of them as they occur, we do not experience them fully; we merely become engrossed in thoughts *about* them. There is no freedom in that. If we are attached to what is seen, heard, tasted, smelt, touched, remembered or anticipated, then we place ourselves in bondage.

From moment to moment we should be aware of what is going on within ourselves. If desire springs up, we should acknowledge it as desire and then let it go. If hatred springs up, we should do likewise — acknowledge its presence, and then let it go. Fear, hope, worry, wishful thinking, daydreaming or any emotional state should be treated in the same way — being aware of its presence and then letting it go.

Being unattached to circumstances and conditions may be easier than being unattached to people. We should be aware of the way we react to what others say and do. If we are attached to their words and deeds, we are not free. There is no need for us to suffer because others are moody or unkind. They are entitled to be the way they want to be. If only we can accept the fact that we do not have to feel ill will towards those who do not act in the way we would act ourselves, then we shall be saved a lot of suffering and so will they. If we note the way we react to others and then let those thoughts and feelings go, we shall retain the natural freedom of our hearts and minds, and the natural freedom of this moment.

Attachment is the root cause of suffering; nonattachment is freedom from it. Nonattachment, however, does *not* mean aloof indifference.

THIS MOMENT

If we only have an intellectual understanding of what is meant by being aware in this moment, then we might think that this moment is 'now' and 'now' and 'now'. We might think these 'nows' have been coming from time immemorial and will continue to do so on into an endless future — an enormous chain of 'nows'. But is this our experience? Do we really experience lots of 'nows'? The truth of the matter is we do not even experience one 'now'. Our experience of this moment is free of time, it is free of 'now'.

Transcending time and space —
Here we are!

When we are truly aware, we shall realize that this moment neither begins nor ends. In true awareness we cannot even describe it as 'now'.

Being aware of this moment as it is, is the point of all the Buddha's teachings. This moment, free from beginning and ending, is Buddha.

THE MIDDLE WAY.

This unborn, undying moment may also be referred to as the Middle Way.

. . the Middle Way consists in not creating hardships for yourself and on the other hand not indulging to your heart's content in sensual pleasures.   Walking the Middle Way brings about conditions in every way conducive to study and practice, and to success in putting an end to suffering.   The expression 'Middle Way' can be applied generally in many and varied situations.   It can't lead you astray.   The Middle Way consists in striking the golden mean.   Knowing causes, knowing effects, knowing oneself, knowing how much is enough, knowing the right company, knowing people: these noble virtues constitute walking the Middle Way.

Buddhadasa Bhikkhu
Buddha Dhamma for Students

SKILFUL MEANS

Skilful means is skilful living.   When we pay attention to what is happening we shall become very receptive to all situations.   In awareness we shall know how to act in order to retain our freedom of mind.   In this way we shall do what is appropriate for others, at the same time avoiding mental defilements and their karmic reactions. If jealousy, anger, hatred or any unwholesome feelings or states of mind arise, it is skilful to let them go immediately and not to allow them to spring forth into words and actions which carry us into unhappiness.

Fault-finding is another major source of conflict in our lives and it would be unskilful to participate in it. If we avoid grumbling, criticizing and finding fault, then we shall be using skilful means. Living skilfully is living spontaneously, unrestricted by set rules or habits, being free of wishful thinking, attachment and aversion, and thereby being free of delusion and suffering.

WISDOM AND COMPASSION

When we do not fritter away our energy into unskilful self-centred mental activity and emotional states, that energy will automatically be channelled into wisdom and compassion.

In selflessness we are wise; in selflessness we are compassionate. Being aware of life as it is, not blocking out the world's woe by self-centred thought and emotion is being wise and compassionate. And wisdom and compassion are the natural expressions of our Buddha-nature, our true nature.

ENLIGHTENMENT

Enlightenment is the opposite of ignorance. To be enlightened is to be undeluded by false notions, views, opinions, beliefs or desires; it is to be unfooled by appearances and to be awakened to truth. Once we realize that the body is impermanent and not self, and that thoughts are impermanent and not self, then we shall simultaneously realize our Buddha-nature.

When the truth of impermanence is fully seen, then it will be realized that 'self' is just a word rather than an identifiable reality. This realization is liberation and release from suffering.

Not to be ignorant is to be enlightened. All one has to do in order to abandon ignorance is to live in a nonharming wise and compassionate way. Such a way of life is true happiness. We may live in a deluded way; or in an enlightened way — the choice is entirely ours.

When selfishness really hurts,
then the Path is easy.

THE GOOD LAW

The ancient Indians loved to analyse holy works and classify them into set formulas and lists. As time went by, the teachings of the Buddha underwent this process and hence we have many numerical presentations of the teaching. Here are just a few:

Three Characteristics of Existence

Unsatisfactoriness, impermanence and not-self.

Three Gates to Liberation

Emptiness
Freedom from all notions of self.

Wishlessness
Freedom from all forms of grasping, desiring, etc.

Signlessness (Causelessness)
Freedom from greed, hatred and delusion.

Threefold Training for Enlightenment

Morality, meditation and wisdom.
All three are interrelated and inter-dependent.

Three Poisons

Greed, hatred and delusion.
The Buddha called these the three
poisons because they poison the purity
of one's true nature.

Three Refuges

Buddha, Dharma, Sangha.

Four Noble Truths

Suffering
Birth is suffering; old age, death,
sorrow, misery, grief and despair
are suffering; association with those
one does not like is suffering; separation
from those one likes is suffering; not
getting what one desires is suffering.

The Origin of Suffering
Craving, desiring, grasping and
attachment are the cause of suffering.

The Cessation of Suffering
When craving ceases, suffering ceases.

*The Path which is the Cessation
of Suffering*
The Eightfold Path is the way which is
free of suffering. (See Eightfold Path.)

Four Attachments

> *Attachment to sense objects, wrong views, rule and ritual, and the word 'self'.*

Four Means of Conversion

> *Giving, kind words, helpfulness, and consistency between words and deeds.*

Four Perverted Views

> *One mistakes the impermanent for the permanent, ill for ease, not-self for self, and the repulsive for the lovely.*

Four Sublime States

> *Loving kindness, compassion, sympathetic joy, and equanimity.*

Four Universal Vows of a Bodhisattva

> *No matter how many beings there are, I vow to liberate them.*

> *No matter how great the defilements are, I vow to purify them.*

No matter how deep the teaching of the Buddha is, I vow to master it.

No matter how incomparable Buddha-nature is, I vow to realize it.

Five Aggregates

Form, feeling, perception, mental activity, and consciousness.
These five constituent parts of existence are erroneously regarded as permanent and self, when in actuality they are impermanent and not self.

Five Aids to Liberation

Faith, vigour, mindfulness, concentration, and wisdom.

Five Hindrances to Liberation

Sense desire, doubt, ill will, sloth and torpor, agitation and anxiety.

Five Precepts (Protections against sorrow)

To refrain from injury to living beings.

To refrain from taking that which
is not freely given.

To refrain from immorality.

To refrain from false or malicious
speech.

To refrain from intoxicating drink
and drugs.

Six Perfections

To give without selfish motive.

To be moral without self-righteousness.

To patiently accept life as it is.

To be vigorous in treading the Path.

To be aware of every action of body,
speech and mind.

To act wisely on all occasions.

Seven Limbs of Enlightenment

Mindfulness, investigation, vigour,
joyous zest, tranquillity, concentration,
and evenmindedness.

Eightfold Path

Right Understanding
To understand the Four Noble Truths.

Right Thought
To refrain from putting two thoughts
together to form a view; to refrain
from attaching to views and opinions.

Right Speech
To abstain from lying, gossiping, and
speaking unnecessarily or harshly.

Right Action
To keep the Five Precepts.

Right Livelihood
To maintain one's livelihood without
harming any living being.

Right Effort
To make the effort to remain aware
and unattached in all circumstances.

Right Mindfulness
To be aware of all that one does in
thought, speech and action.

Right Concentration
To remain free of all mental disturb-
ances, such as worry, anxiety, envy, etc.

Ten Fetters which Chain One to Sorrow

> *Belief in a self, attachment to rules*
> *and rituals, doubts about the teaching,*
> *greed for sense pleasures, attachment*
> *to form, attachment to emptiness,*
> *ill will, excited mind or thoughts,*
> *conceit, and ignorance.*

Twelve Links of Dependent Origination

This is a way of illustrating how it
is possible to fall into the delusion
of existence.

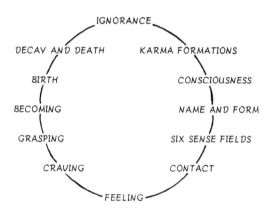

The chain is made up of false notions
and unwise actions which follow on
one from the other, leading round
and round, back and forth. The chain
may be broken anywhere by insight.
For example, if we realize there is
no birth, then at that moment there
is no ignorance, no karma formations
. . . no decay and no death.

QUESTIONS AND ANSWERS

Q: Do Buddhists worship images?

A: To most Buddhists, East and West,
Buddha-rupas (forms) are not considered to
be more than just stone, wood or metal
objects. They are reminders that Buddha
was a man who presented a teaching to help
mankind.

In the East, bowing has always been
customary as a sign of respect. It is not
surprising, therefore, that it became customary to bow before Buddha-rupas as a sign
of respect for the teaching. This bowing
does not signify worship.

It was at least five hundred years after
the time of the Buddha before rupas came
into existence. Prior to that an empty
space or a footprint was used to represent
the Buddha, or a wheel to represent the
teaching.

Q: Do Buddhists believe in God?

A: Buddhism is nontheistic. There is no God in Buddhism in the way that God in Christianity is commonly understood.

Q: How does one become a Buddhist?

A: By adopting a Buddhist way of life.

Q: Does one have to be a vegetarian in order to be a Buddhist?

A: There are no prerequisites to taking up a Buddhist way of life. The basis of Buddhism, however, is nonharming, compassion, wisdom, and awareness of body, speech and mind. Once the path is taken up, it is difficult to mindfully eat the bodies of other sentient beings. Vegetarianism, as well as other harmless ways of life, is therefore a natural consequence of treading the Buddhist path.

Q: Is it necessary to choose and follow a particular school of Buddhism?

A: We may join a group and learn from others, but if we become sectarian and proud, then we shall only add to our delusion. The Dharma (truth, the teaching of the Buddha) is beyond words and form. If one inclines to enlightenment, help and direction in treading the path will naturally ensue. The path is one's life. There is no need to pick and choose. The way lies straight ahead at all times.

The perfect way is difficult only for those who pick and choose . . .

Seng-t'san
On Trust in the Heart
and Believing in Mind

MAJOR BUDDHIST SCHOOLS

The following is a brief account of some of the Buddhist schools existing in the world today. Not all of the sects and subsects have been mentioned as they are too numerous and complex for a book of this kind.

CH'AN

Ch'an (lit. meditation) exists to a limited degree in Korea, Singapore, Hong Kong and China. Like other religions in China, Buddhism was repressed during the cultural revolution. There are signs now, however, of its reanimation.

The body of Hui Neng the Sixth Ch'an/Zen Patriarch
in his monastery at Ts'ao Ch'i.

Ch'an, like most forms of Buddhism, is very direct, emphasizing the importance of realizing truth 'in this moment'. Its main practice is nonattachment.

In approximately AD 1200 this form of Buddhism spread to Japan and became known as Zen. In the West that which is commonly referred to as Zen, is in fact Ch'an.

If we allow our thoughts, past, present, and future, to link up in a series, we put ourselves under restraint. On the other hand, if we never let our minds attach to anything, we shall gain emancipation. For this reason, we take 'Nonattachment' as our fundamental principle.

Wong Mou-Lam (trans.)
The Sutra of Hui Neng

The way is perfect and complete
like boundless space;
nothing is lacking, nothing redundant,
but, because the mind continues to
make distinctions,
its Suchness is obscured.

Seng-t'san
On Trust in the Heart
and Believing in Mind

Recommended Reading:
"The Sutra of Hui Neng", trans. Wong Mou-Lam, in *The Diamond Sutra and the Sutra of Hui Neng*, Shambhala Publications Inc., Colorado, U.S.A. 1969.

PURE LAND

Pure Land Buddhism is practised mainly in Japan (there are several sects), but the idea of a refuge or Buddha-land is found in almost every school of Buddhism. In the very earliest parts of the Pali Canon (the collection of the scriptures of the Theravada School), Nirvana was often described as a place or island of refuge. The idea of a Pure Land also exists in Tibetan Buddhism.

Pure Land Buddhism is based on the forty-eight vows of Hozo Bosatsu (Skt. Dharmakara Bodhisattva) who became Amida Buddha* (Skt. Amitabha), the most important of which is the eighteenth:

When I have obtained Buddhahood, if those beings who are in the ten quarters, after they have heard my name, should direct their thoughts towards my country and should plant the roots of merit (or prepare their stock of merit), and should bring them to maturity with their serene thoughts, and wish to be born in my country, — if they

* A spiritual (not material) Buddha. From an historical point of view there is only one Buddha, Siddhartha Gautama, in another sense, however, there are many Buddhas. The word 'Buddha' means awakened. Everyone has the capability of becoming awakened and becoming Buddha. In a sense, therefore, there are as many potential Buddhas as there are beings and as many Buddhas as there are awakened beings.

*should not accomplish (their desire), may I
not obtain the perfect knowledge.*

F. Max Muller (ed.)
"The Larger Sukhavati-Vyuha"
Sacred Books of the East Vol. XLIX

What distinguishes this School of Buddhism from the others is the recitation of the
mantra (known as the Nembutsu):

NAMU AMIDA BUTSU

(Japanese)

A-MI-T'O-FO

(Chinese)

*Contemplating Amida Buddha,
saying his name.*

Calling upon Amida Buddha in this way
is said to cause one to be reborn in the Pure
Land where it is easy to realize enlightenment.

To some, this School seems to be a contradiction of the Buddha's (Siddhartha
Gautama s) teaching because of its seeming
reliance on faith and outside help.   It is,
however, only a contradiction if one con-
siders that the Pure Land is outside of oneself or if one confuses faith with belief.
The recitation of a mantra which brings to
mind the Buddha will clear the mind of
discursive thought and inspire it to the good.
This is the Pure Land where enlightenment
is easy.

The man who rejoices in true faith
is equal to the Tathagata —
Great faith is none other than
Buddha-nature
And Buddha-nature is Tathagata.

Shinran Shonin
Shinran in the Contemporary World

Recommended Reading:

"The Larger Sukhavati-Vyuha" and "The Smaller Sukhavati-Vyuha", trans. F. Max Muller, and "The Amitayur-Dhyana-Sutra", trans. J. Takakusa, in Vol. XLIX of *Sacred Books of the East.* Motilal Banarsidass, Delhi. 1965.

Tanni Sho, trans. Kenju Masuyama and Professor Ryosetsu Fujiwara, Ryukoku Translation Series Vol. II, Ryukoku University, Kyoto. 1963.

THERAVADA

The Buddhism of Sri Lanka, Burma and Thailand encompasses numerous branches and subsects which differ in many ways. In the West, however, they are usually all simply referred to as Theravada.

Thera means elder and a Theravadin is one established in the way of the elders. It is a popular school in the West and was thought by early Western Buddhists to be the 'original' Buddhism.

The cornerstone of Theravada Buddhism is the relationship between the monks and the lay people. The role of the monk is to live the religious life. The role of the lay person is to support and help the monk with food, etc. It is a way of mutual support: the lay person gives material support to the monk, the monk gives spiritual support to the lay person. The system does not exclude the lay person from putting the teaching into practice. There are many lay people who go very deeply into the teaching.

In most Theravada countries, at least one young man of every Buddhist family would be encouraged to become a monk. This practice was common in many other Buddhist countries as well. Buddhist monks do not take life vows and it

Moggallana

is quite acceptable to be a monk for a short while only.

The wise are restrained
in body, speech, and mind —
they are perfectly restrained.

The Dhammapada, v. 234

For those with preferences, suffering is in-
evitable, since love and hate depend upon
each other; when there is one there is the
other.

Ven. Achaan Brahmamuni
The Burdened Heart

Recommended Reading:

The Dhammapada, Jack Austin, The Buddhist
Society, London.

The Middle Length Sayings, Vols. I, II and III,
trans. I.B. Horner, The Pali Text Society.

TIBETAN

There are several sects of Tibetan Buddhism,
the main ones being the Nyingmapa, the
Kadampa, the Kagyupa, the Sakyapa and the
Gelukpa. In Tibet, as in Theravada countries,
there was a strong relationship between lay
people and monks.

It was both traditional and honourable
for men and women to become ordained.
Added to this, and quite unique to Tibetan
Buddhism, was as system whereby young
children were 'recognized' as incarnations
(tulkus) of High Lamas. Perhaps the most
famous of these *tulkus,* or recognized Lamas,
is the Dalai Lama (the spiritual and secular

leader of the Tibetan people), who is believed to be the reincarnation of Chenrezig (Skt. Avalokiteshvara), the Bodhisattva of Compassion.

Tibet no longer exists as an independent country. The Chinese occupation of 1950 led to the flight of the XIV Dalai Lama to India in 1959 with thousands of Tibetans. However, some traditions and practices have survived with the refugees and it is in relation to these refugees that we may now talk of Tibetan Buddhism.

Tibetan Buddhism is based on the relationship between teacher *(guru)* and disciple or student. The student is taught to honour and respect his guru at all times. Buddhist scholarship and art are held in very high regard and years are spent undergoing courses of study and practice. The teacher carefully gauges the progress of the student and when appropriate, ceremonies are performed, initiating the student into tantric rituals and practices.

In its noblest sense, the guru ideal is related to anyone or anything. An enemy may be a guru if one learns patience as a result of encountering him. Humiliation may be a guru if one learns humility as a result of it. Anything and everything may be a guru to the truly devout person: sounds, sights, sensations, feelings, emotions, thoughts — in fact all that one experiences in life.

His Holiness Dalai Lama
On one occasion the Dalai Lama was heard to say,
'People ask me what my religion is. I tell them,
my religion is kindness.'

As in all schools of Buddhism, Tibetan practices, rituals, mantras and mandalas have a common purpose, i.e. to point out that it is ignorance which obstructs the realization of truth.

A few Tibetan teachers have established centres in the West and this kind of Buddhism has now become very popular.

Act so that ye have no cause to be ashamed of yourselves; and hold fast to this rule.

Milarepa
(ed.) W.Y. Evans-Wentz
Tibet's Great Yogi Milarepa

A common mantra:

OM MANI PADME HUM

'Hail to the jewel in the lotus!'

or

*'Hail to the splendour (or Buddha)
of your own mind!'*

*Those who see into their true nature,
Are instantaneously initiated
Into all the mystic teachings.*

Recommended Reading:

Tibet's Great Yogi Milarepa, ed. W.Y. Evans-Wentz, Oxford University Press, London.

The Opening of the Wisdom Eye, H.H. The XIV Dalai Lama, The Social Science Association Press of Thailand.

ZEN

Zen is the Japanese form of Buddhism which is similar to Ch'an from which it developed. It has two main schools — Rinzai and Soto.

In meditation, koans (Zen sayings) are used, particularly in the Rinzai sect, as a means of breaking through the barrier of ignorance which stands in the way of truth. These koans are expressions of the Zen Masters which at first may seem strange or nonsensical.

Once a monk made a request of Joshu. 'I have just entered the monastery,' he said. 'Please give me instructions, Master.' Joshu said, 'Have you had your breakfast?' 'Yes, I have,' replied the monk. 'Then,' said Joshu, 'wash your bowls.' The monk had an insight.
Zenkei Shibayama
Zen Comments on the Mumonkan

The cornerstone of Zen Buddhism is a disciplined practice in daily life, of work and meditation.   It is a very popular form of Buddhism in the West.

True study of the Way does not rely on knowledge and genius or cleverness and brilliance.   But it is a mistake to encourage people to be like blind men, deaf mutes, or imbeciles.   Because study [of the Way] has no use for wide learning and high intelligence, even those with inferior capacities can participate.   True study of the Way is an easy thing.

Dogen
Reiho Masunaga (trans.)
A Primer of Soto Zen

Recommended Reading:

Zen Comments on the Mumonkan, Zenkei Shibayama, Harper & Row, San Francisco.

A Primer of Soto Zen, Reiho Masunaga, Routledge & Kegan Paul, London.

Benkei Zen, Peter Haskel, Grove Press, Inc., New York.

HINAYANA/MAHAYANA

Hinayana and Mahayana are not schools of Buddhism, though they are often referred to as such.

'Yana' means 'vehicle', 'career', 'way', or 'way through' (to liberation). 'Hinayana' means 'small vehicle' and is the way of those who listen to the teaching but do not fully put that teaching into practice. 'Mahayana' means 'great vehicle' and is the way of those who listen to the teaching and then practise it.

> *Few are those who cross over*
> *the stream of birth and death.*
> *Most just run up and down*
> *on this shore.*
>
> The Dhammapada, v. 85

A misunderstanding of these terms will lead to great confusion. Hinayana has been equated with Theravada Buddhism and Mahayana with schools such as Tibetan and Zen. This is an error.

When the Buddhist movement split in about 340 BC, the Theravada schools did not exist, nor did the Zen and Tibetan schools. The split was among scholars and commentators in regard to such matters as 'existence', 'nonexistence', 'the nature of reality', and 'the behaviour of Arhats' etc. It should not be thought that those who put the teaching into practice find any essential differences in the scriptures of any school.

The terms Hinayana and Mahayana really refer to the way the individual practises rather than to the school to which that person belongs. A Hinayanist is one who rides in the small vehicle and treads the lower path, while, a Mahayanist is one who rides in the great vehicle and treads the higher path. A follower of the Theravada (the so-called Hinayana) tradition who puts the teaching into practice is a Mahayanist, while a follower of the Zen or Tibetan traditions (the so-called Mahayana) who does not put the teaching into practice is a Hinayanist, and vice versa.

When new schools or sects were founded or established, it was generally as a reaction to previous corruptions. It is unlikely that the Buddha would have intended schools and sects to have developed in the first place. Indeed, it is unlikely he would have called himself 'a Buddhist, the founder of a religion' It could be said that the mere fact Buddhism has become a formalized religion is a corruption in itself. The Buddha denounced the corruptions of established religions in India and even went so far as to say that attachment to rites and rituals was a hindrance to enlightenment. He wanted people to understand the truth of their own hearts and minds, rather than to become members of any set religion.

Another example of this attitude (one of many) was given by Dogen (c.1225) who,

although accredited as being the founder of
Soto Zen in Japan, himself refused to be
sectarian.

Attachment to views
is the cause of all suffering —
don't let sectarianism
defile your Buddha-nature.

ADVICE ON TREADING THE PATH

There are many schools of Buddhism and
they all present the teaching in their own
ways. We in the West are fortunate in that
we have the opportunity of studying these
different interpretations of the Buddha's
teaching. Sometimes it is useful to have the
same thing explained in a variety of ways,
as it may help us to realize the essential
reality to which they all refer.

Buddhism is a way of life, not just a set
of doctrines. If we only learn the teaching
(or worse still become sectarian in our out-
look) we can never hope to really understand
the freedom of mind that Buddhism offers.

The Buddha was once in a town called
Kalama, where he was asked, 'What is the
best way of knowing if a religious teaching
is true or not?' To which the Buddha replied, 'Do not be swayed by tradition, nor by
scripture, nor by established principles. Do

not believe a teaching just because you have heard it many times, or because you believe it to be true, or because you have surmised or reasoned that it is true. Nor should you base the truth upon someone else's seeming ability or attainment, nor out of respect for that person if he is your teacher.

'Kalamas, when you know for yourselves that a certain action of body, speech or mind is unskilful, blameworthy, unwise, then abandon that action.

'The same criteria should be used to judge what is right. If an action of body, speech or mind is without blame and is the wise thing to do, then cultivate it, practise it, abide in that way of life.

'Kalamas, see for yourselves whether or not greed, hatred or self-centred actions lead to misery. If they do, then abandon them.

'See for yourselves, Kalamas, whether or not nonattachment, compassion and kindness lead to happiness for both yourselves and for others. If they do, then practise them, do not abandon them, base your way of life on them, and you will soon know the truth.'

Adapted from the Kalama Sutta
Anguttara Nikaya

Live as lamps to yourselves, as refuges to yourselves, with no other refuges.

The Buddha
Maha-Parinibbana Suttanta
Digha-Nikaya

Religion in everyday language is temples, monastery buildings, pagodas, yellow robes and so on; religion in Dhamma language is the Truth which can really serve man as a point of support.

Buddhadasa Bhikkhu
Two Kinds of Language

CHRONOLOGICAL HISTORY

There is very little factual evidence relating to the first four or five hundred years of Buddhist history. What information does exist is based on accounts written long after the events. Dates are more accurate after the first five hundred years mainly because the Chinese meticulously recorded such details.

*c.*550 BC

The birth of Siddhartha Gautama, later to be known as the Buddha. In Sri Lanka the dates given are 623-543 BC and in Thailand 624-544 BC. Most Western scholars favour 566-486 BC or 563-483 BC. (See: 274-236 BC. The reign of King Asoka.)

The First Council at Rajagriha was said to have taken place shortly after the passing of the Buddha. Ananda, one of the Buddha's disciples, is believed to have recited the teaching and Upali, another disciple, is believed to have recited the Rules of the Order (the *Vinaya*).

Prior to the formation of any sects or schools of Buddhism, groups assembled. Very little is known about these groups apart from their names. Some had place names such as East Rock; some were named after districts or people; and others had names like Lucky Vehicle and Those who Guard the Dharma.

c.340 BC

The Second Council at Vaisali. A split in the *Sangha* (Buddhist Order) later developed into two main schools: the Mahasanghikas and the Sthaviras.

Developments from the Sthaviras were the Pudgalavadins (*c*.280 BC) — as a reaction against the dogmatism of no-self, — the Vibhajyavadins and the Sarvastivadins (*c*. 244 BC). The Theravada School of Sri Lanka probably developed as or from a subsect of the Vibhajyavadins. The Sarvastivadins were for a long time the main Buddhist School in India and it is probable that the early Buddhism of Thailand was the Sarvastivadins or a branch of that School. Some of these early schools became very intellectual and there arose a school called the Sautrantikas as a reaction.

For hundreds of years after these 'splits', monks of different schools often shared the same monasteries and the same scriptures. It was only their more technical books (such as the Abhidhamma) which were not shared.

From the Mahasanghikas the Madhyamika, Yogacarin, Tantric, Pure Land, Zen and Tibetan forms of Buddhism eventually developed. These developments took hundreds of years. There were many overlaps. One of Tibet's foremost Tantric teachers, Gampopa (AD 1079-1153), for example, was a Sarvastivadin monk. Some of these schools were also popular in Sri Lanka. Vasubandhu (c. AD 450) was a Sarvastivadin as well as a Yogacarin. And Nagarjuna (c. AD 150) is considered to be the patriarch of virtually every school of Buddhism.*

274-236 BC

The reign of King Asoka, who was a powerful warrior and who instigated the most terrible wars. In time he became disgusted by the horrors of those wars and was converted to Buddhism. Abolishing wars and all unnecessary killing for food, he propagated Buddhism in India as well as abroad, sending

* Although not a patriarch of the Theravada School, Nagarjuna is said to have had a strong influence over Buddhaghosa c.450 who is considered to be the 'father' of modern Theravada Buddhism.

emissaries to countries such as Sri Lanka, Egypt and possibly even to Greece.

King Asoka had a great influence on early Buddhism. At his command, Buddhist edicts were etched upon stone tablets and pillars throughout India, many of which have survived the centuries.

The dates given for the reign of this King are fairly accurate. In fact they are the only reasonably accurate dates up to this time. Prior to this, accounts were vague and are difficult to place on any time scale. By using this period as a reference point, historians have been able to date earlier Buddhist history. Even the dates given for the Buddha's life were plotted from this period.

During the reign of Asoka, a Third Council may have taken place at Patna, though there are doubts about this.

c.250 BC
Buddhism introduced into Sri Lanka by Mahinda and Sanghamitta, believed to be the son and daughter of King Asoka.

c.200 BC
Buddhism spread to Central Asia.

c.100 BC

From the time of the Buddha up to this period, it is not known in which language the teaching was transmitted. The Buddha himself stressed that all teaching should be in the local dialects of the people concerned so that no one would have difficulty in understanding it. This is undoubtedly what happened. In the course of time, however, the teaching was written down and at some stage committed to various languages including Sanskrit and Pali.* It is not known when this first took place. It may have been about this time, or it may have been earlier.

Legend has it that in Sri Lanka, owing to war and famine, the *Sangha* (Buddhist Order) was in danger of coming to an end. This meant that the teaching, having only been transmitted orally up to this time, was also in danger of coming to an end. Therefore it was written down, the texts in Pali and the Commentaries in Sri Lankan.

How much of the present Pali Canon was written at this time is unknown. Parts of the Sutta-Nipata are reputed to be the oldest.

Around this time texts also existed in Sanskrit. Parts of the Prajna-paramita sutras were in existence, though again it is unknown as to how much.

* Modern scholarship has proved beyond doubt that the earliest texts were in neither Sanskrit nor Pali.

c. AD 50
Buddhism began to spread into China.

c.70
The Fourth Council.

c.100
Asvaghosha, a famous Indian Buddhist, wrote one of the earliest life stories of the Buddha in verse.

 The first Buddha-rupas (forms) came into being. Prior to this time the Buddha was represented by an empty space or a footprint, or his teaching was represented by a wheel.

c.150
Nagarjuna, a famous Indian Buddhist philosopher and patriarch, established the Madhyamika (Middle Doctrine) School of Buddhism.

180
The Vimalakirtinirdesa Sutra was translated from Sanskrit into Chinese. The Indians did not seem to care too much about dates and so there is no record of when this famous Sutra was originally written.

c.300-400
Almost all the knowledge we have today on
the early history of Buddhism (the first five
hundred years) is based upon two Sri Lankan
Chronicles — the Dipavamsa and the Maha-
vamsa. Both were compiled during this
period.

344-413
Kumarajiva travelled from India to China
and translated over three hundred works into
Chinese, including the Lotus Sutra, the Dia-
mond Sutra and the Large Perfection of
Wisdom Sutra.

c.350
Buddhism spread to Korea from China.

c.400
Buddhism spread to Cambodia and Indonesia.

c.400-450
Buddhism spread to Burma and Java.

c.450
Buddhaghosa, a famous Indian Buddhist,
translated Sri Lankan Commentaries into
Pali. He also compiled the Visuddhi Magga
(Path of Purity).

The Pali Canon was revised and finalized in Sri Lanka.

The Theravada School as it is today probably dates from this period.

The Buddhist University of Nalanda in India was established.

Asanga, with his (said) brother Vasubandhu established the Yogacara (Mind Only) School of Buddhism in India.

c.500
The rise of Tantra (mysticism and ritualistic rites) in India which had a great effect on both Buddhism and Hinduism.

The Pure Land School was established in China.

c.520
Bodhidharma travelled from India to China and founded the Ch'an/Zen School.

c.550
Buddhism spread to Japan from Korea.

596-664
Hiuen Tsiang, a Chinese monk, left China in 630 for India in search of scriptures and returned in 644 with many Buddhist works. He spent the rest of his life translating many of them (over seventy) into Chinese.

His journey to India became a legend, later to become the basis of an epic story by Wu Ch'eng-en (*c.*1505-80). In this story Hiuen Tsiang was referred to as Tripitaka. (See *Monkey*, trans. Arthur Waley, Unwin Paperbacks.)

610
Buddhism became the state religion in Japan.

638-713
Hui Neng, the Sixth Chinese Ch'an/Zen Patriarch, popularised Ch'an Buddhism in China.

c.640
Buddhism spread to Tibet.

c.720
Buddhism spread to Thailand. There is a degree of uncertainty about this date. The Thais may have brought Buddhism with them when they migrated from their homeland (today part of China).

c.750
Padmasambhava, an Indian Buddhist who travelled to Tibet, is said to have founded the Nyingmapa sect.

767-822
Dengyo Daishi founded the Tendai sect in Japan.

793-4
The Council of bSam Yas, Tibet, took place to decide whether to adopt Pala Buddhism from India or Ch'an Buddhism from China as the official religion for Tibet. Pala Buddhism got its name from the Pala dynasty centred around Bengal 750-1150. This is the form of Buddhism that was chosen.

c.800
Copper plates in Sri Lanka were inscribed with parts of the Prajnaparamita Sutras in Sri Lankan script (the Indikutasaya Copper Plates). At this time several schools of Buddhism and Tantra existed in Sri Lanka alongside the Theravada schools.

?-867
Lin-chi (Chin.), Rinzai (Jap.), a Ch'an/Zen Master lived in China and founded the School which bears his name.

868
The oldest known printed book in the world, a Chinese copy of the Diamond *(Vajra-cchedika)* Sutra, is now preserved in the British Museum.

c.1012-1087
Marpa, the translator, lived, who made two trips to India for scriptures and founded the Kagyupa sect in Tibet.

c.1040-1123
Milarepa, a disciple of Marpa, was one of Tibet's greatest teachers. For his life story see *Tibet's Great Yogi Milarepa*, ed. W.Y. Evans-Wentz, Oxford University Press, Oxford.

c.1100
Burma began to adopt the Sri Lankan form of Theravada Buddhism.

1133-1212
Honen Shonin lived and established the *(Jodo)* Pure Land School of Buddhism in Japan.

1173-1262
Shinran Shonin (a disciple of Honen) lived and founded the Jodo-Shin sect in Japan.

1191
Japanese Zen Master Eisai (1141-1215) went to China and brought Rinzai Zen (Chin. Linchi) back to Japan.

c.1197
The Buddhist University of Nalanda in India was destroyed along with many Buddhist texts by the Mohammedans. Most of the Buddhist Sanskrit literature comes down to us today because it was preserved in Tibet and China. The Pali texts were preserved in Sri Lanka.

c.1200-1400
Buddhism in India declined dramatically.

c.1225
Japanese Zen Master Dogen (1200-1253) travelled to China and brought Soto Zen (Chin. Ts'ao-tung) back to Japan.

Buddhism spread to Mongolia and Siberia.

1252
The Great Buddha (Amida in meditation) was erected at Kamakura, Japan. Constructed of bronze plates welded together it stands at fifty-two feet high. The building in which it was originally housed was demolished by an enormous tidal wave.

The Great Buddha in Kamakura, Japan.
Amida in meditation.

1300
The Sri Lankan form of Buddhism was established in Thailand. Prior to this there were various Buddhist schools in Thailand.

c.1350
Buddhism spread to Laos.

1360
Buddhism became the official religion of Thailand.

1357-1419
Tsongkhapa founded the Gelukpa sect in Tibet.

1411
The Kanjur (Tibetan Canon) was printed for the first time in Peking.

c.1600
Buddhism began to decline in Japan and in 1769 Shintoism became the state religion.

c.1600-1800
Buddhism began to decline in Sri Lanka. Monks had to be imported from Burma and Thailand in order to keep the Sangha (Order

of monks) going. At one time it is said there were fewer than five monks on the island. (In a census of 1971 it was established there were 18,670 monks.)

c.1642
The Potala was built in Lhasa, Tibet.

1685-1768
Zen Master Hakuin, a famous Japanese poet and artist, reformed Zen training and systematized the use of koans. Modern day Zen training in the Rinzai School probably originated from him.

c.1800
Buddhism spread to the West.

1879
The publication of the well known book *The Light of Asia* by Sir Edwin Arnold, (Routledge & Kegan Paul, London), which is an account of the Buddha's life and teaching in verse.

c.1880
Buddhism in Sri Lanka was revived by the Theosophical Society.

1891

The Maha Bodhi Society was founded in Calcutta by a Sri Lankan Buddhist.

1907

The Buddhist Society of Great Britain and Ireland was formed in London. It was replaced by the Buddhist League in 1923 and disbanded in 1925.

1924

The Buddhist Lodge, London, was formed, which later became The Buddhist Society.

1929

Les Amis du Bouddhisme, Paris, was formed.

1930

The First Zen Institute, New York, was formed.

c.1950 to date

Many Buddhist centres, groups, temples and monasteries have been established throughout the Western world.

It is difficult to calculate how many Buddhists there are in the West today. Buddhism is not a religion which demands any outward show and, although many join groups and attend meetings, there are a great number who do not.

There is also a large number who combine Buddhism with other religions, never feeling the need to make a conscious choice between them.

The Buddhapadipa Temple
A Thai temple in Wimbledon, London.

What is the future of Buddhism?   No one can say.   However, as long as there are people suffering, it will have a place.

I, Buddh, who wept with all my
brothers' tears,
Whose heart was broken
by a whole world's woe,
Laugh and am glad,
for there is Liberty!
Ho! ye who suffer! Know

Ye suffer from yourselves.
None else compels,
None other holds you
that ye live and die,
And whirl upon the wheel,
and hug and kiss
Its spokes of agony,

The Light of Asia
Sir Edwin Arnold

GLOSSARY OF BUDDHIST TERMS

Abhidhamma
Lit. Further dhamma. A highly analytical collection of Buddhist works on psychology and philosophy. Name of the third section of Buddhist writings (the first being the Sutras and the second being the *Vinaya*).

Amida (Jap.), Amitabha (Skt.)
Unmeasured splendour; the personification of compassion symbolized as the Buddha of Infinite Light or *Amitayus* (Skt.) the Buddha of Infinite Life.

Anatta
Not self. One of the three characteristics of existence.

Anicca
Impermanence, transience, as evidenced by old age, disease, and death. One of the three characteristics of existence.

Arahat (Skt.), Arahant (P.)
A person who has liberated himself from all defilements and impurities.

Ariyan
Noble, pure, flawless, supermundane.

Awareness
The simple observation of whatever is taking place in this moment. Being quite free of discursive thought (q.v.). Being open to life, allowing it to flow naturally without obstruction.

Bodhi
Awakening, understanding, perfect wisdom; the illuminated or enlightened mind.

Bodhicitta
Thought which is awakened; the awakened mind; the mental attitude which aspires to Buddhahood or Bodhisattvahood.

Bodhisattva
One who inclines towards Enlightenment; one who vows to liberate all beings from Samsara.

Bodhi Tree
The tree under which the Buddha attained Enlightenment; a symbol of Enlightenment.

Buddha
One who is awakened; Siddhartha Gautama became awakened to truth and was thenceforth known as the Buddha.

Buddha-nature
The essence of what one really is; one's true nature.

Buddha-rupa (form)
Statue representing the Buddha.

Citta
Mind, thought or consciousness.

Compassion (Skt. Karuna)
Selfless love; total unity with the suffering of all beings.

Deathless
That which is not born and does not die; a synonym for Nirvana.

Defilement
(See Klesa.)

Devas/Devatas
The heavenly or shining ones, the gods.

Buddha-rupa
at The Buddhapadipa Temple, Wimbledon, London.

Dharma (Skt.), Dhamma (P.)
The teaching of the Buddha; that which supports reality; the truth; the natural state.

Dharmakaya
Body of truth; reality.

Discursive Thought
The opposite of awareness. Argumentative type thought — worrying, doubting, hoping, always weighing the balance between this and that.

Dukkha
Sorrow; the pain of ignorance; the misery of Samsara; that which defiles reality. One of the three characteristics of existence.

Enlightenment
The realization of truth; seeing things as they are; awakening to reality.

Guru
Teacher.

Hinayana
The smaller or lesser vehicle, or way. (See section on Hinayana/Mahayana p. 59.)

Karma
Action and reaction; cause and effect.

Klesa
Delusion, defilement, greed, hatred; that which contaminates the natural purity of one's true nature.

Koan
Sayings and doings of the Zen Masters in which their enlightenment experiences are freely and directly expressed. These koans may at first seem bewildering, incomprehensible statements not amenable to conceptual understanding. When they are 'worked on', however, understanding or realization may arise; then they become perfectly logical, clear expressions of reality.

Lama
A high-ranking Tibetan monk.

Mahayana
The larger or greater vehicle, or way. (See section on Hinayana/Mahayana p. 59.)

Mandala
A sacred circle (a diagram painted, made of coloured sand, or other materials) used in meditation and ceremonies.

Mantra
A sacred formula, incantation; sounds formed orally or mentally to make the mind alert.

Mara
The personification of evil, the Destroyer, the Evil One; defilement, delusion.

Meditation
Union with the real. To be aware without any trace of discursive thought. To see all things for what they are after false views have been cleared away.

Middle Way
A synonym for the Buddha's teaching; transcending all extremes — good and bad, right and wrong, etc; staying exactly in 'this moment'.

Nembutsu
The mantra *Namu Amida Butsu.*

Nirodha
The going down of all suffering which is the realization of Nirvana.

Nirvana (Skt.), Nibbana (P.)
The unborn; the utmost security from the bonds of greed, hatred and delusion; the total extinction of all false views; beyond eternity and annihilation; beyond description and conception; the very basis and foundation of what we are and of all that is; liberation.

Prajna
Wisdom, understanding; the natural functioning of one's Buddha-nature; the function of mindfulness.

Perfection
The total cessation of greed and hatred. The cessation of all delusion. The functioning of one's everyday mind when unblemished by wishing, wanting, hoping, worrying, etc.

Sakyamuni
Sage of the Sakya clan; another name for the Buddha.

Samsara
The round of birth and death; the realms of appearances; the world of suffering.

Sangha
Lit. Community or assembly.
   Bhikkhu-sangha Community of monks.

Suchness (Skt. Tathata)
True state of things, true nature.

Suffering
(See Dukkha.)

Sunyata
Lit. Voidness or Emptiness. The experience
of non-self; experience beyond defilement;
truth devoid of delusion.

Tantra
Lit. Principal part or essence. Texts (and
oral teachings) symbolized in ritual and art
(esp. Vajrayana (Tib.), and Shingon (Jap.)).

Tathagata
Thus come; the one who neither comes nor
goes; one who has attained full enlightenment. Another name for the Buddha and a
name the Buddha often used when referring
to himself.

Tulku
The recognized incarnation of a Lama from a previous existence, who is given the title Rinpoche.

Vajra (Skt.), Dorje (Tib.)
The symbol of supreme power and wisdom.

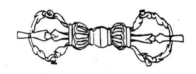

Vajrayana
Name given to the Tantric form of Tibetan Buddhism, sometimes known as Tantrayana.

Vinaya
The rules of discipline for monks, of which there are approximately two hundred and fifty.

Wisdom (Skt. Prajna)
Knowing situations intuitively; knowing how to deal with situations skilfully.

BIBLIOGRAPHY

Arnold, Sir Edwin. 1971. *The Light of Asia*, Routledge & Kegan Paul Ltd, London.

de Bary, W.T., Chan, W. and Watson, B. 1960. *Sources of Chinese Tradition*, Columbia University Press, New York.

Bennett, A.A.G. (trans.). *Long Discourses of the Buddha*, Chetana Ltd, Bombay.

Brahmamuni, Ven. Achaan. 1984. *The Burdened Heart*, Buddhist Publishing Group, Leicester.

Buddhadasa Bhikkhu. B.E. 2526. *Buddha Dhamma for Students*, distributed by Sublime Life Mission, Bangkok.

———. B.E. 2517. *Two Kinds of Language*, distributed by Sublime Life Mission, Bangkok.

Chime Rinpoche, Lama. "The History of Oral Transmission", *Vajra*, Issue No 2, pp. 1-10.

Conze, E. 1975. *The Large Sutra on Perfect Wisdom*, University of California Press, Berkeley.

———. 1980. *A Short History of Buddhism*, George Allen & Unwin, London.

Damrong, H.R.H. Prince. 1971. *Buddhism in Thailand* Information Service of Thailand, London.

The Diamond Sutra, Buddhist Publishing Group, Leicester. 1984.

Edgerton, Professor. 1977. *Buddhist Hybrid Sanskrit Grammar and Dictionary*, Motilal Banarsidass, Delhi.

Ehara, The Rev. N.R.M., Soma Thera and Kheminda Thera. 1977. *The Path of Freedom*, Buddhist Publication Society, Kandy.

Evans-Wentz, W.Y. (ed.). 1969. *Tibet's Great Yogi Milarepa*, Oxford University Press, London.

Gard, R.A. (ed.). 1961. *Buddhism*, Prentice-Hall International, London.

Hazra, Dr K.L. "Religious Intercourse between Ceylon and Siam (Thailand)", *The Maha Bodhi*, July 1972, pp. 341-345.

Horner, I.B. (trans.). 1967. *The Middle Length Sayings (Majjhima-Nikaya)*, Vol. I, The Pali Text Society, London.

Humphreys, C. 1962. *A Popular Dictionary of Buddhism*, Arco Publications, London.

Masunaga, R. 1978. *A Primer of Soto Zen*, Routledge & Kegan Paul, London.

Masuyama, K. and Fujiwara, Professor R. 1963. *The Tanni Sho*, Vol. II, Ryukoku Translation Centre, Ryukoku University, Kyoto.

Monier-Williams, Sir M. 1979. *Sanskrit-English Dictionary*, Oxford University Press, Oxford.

Mou-Lam, W. (trans.). 1969. *The Diamond Sutra and the Sutra of Hui Neng*, Shambhala, Boulder, Colorado.

Muller, F.M. (trans.). 1978 *Buddhist Mahayana Texts*, Sacred Books of the East, Vol. XLIX, Motilal Banarsidass, Delhi.

The Nishi Hongwanji Commission. 1974. *Shinran in the Contemporary World*, Jodo Shinshu Nishi Hongwanji, Kyoto.

Orlandi, E. (ed.), Sugana, G.M., Hart, V. (trans.). 1968. *The Life and Times of Buddha*, Paul Hamlyn, London.

Shibayama, Z. 1975. *Zen Comments on the Mumonkan*, New American Library, New York.

Soothill, Professor W.E. and Hodous, Professor L. 1977. *A Dictionary of Chinese Buddhist Terms*, Motilal Banarsidass, Delhi.

Thomas, E.J. 1971. *The History of Buddhist Thought*, Routledge & Kegan Paul, London.

Tsunoda, R., de Bary, W.T. and Keene, D. 1964. *Sources of Japanese Tradition*, Vol. I, Columbia University Press, New York.

Turner, E. 1982. *On Trust in the Heart and Believing in Mind*, distributed by Buddhist Publishing Group, Leicester.

World Buddhism, Vol. XX, No 6, January 1972. Ceylon.

OTHER BPG PUBLICATIONS

TEACHINGS OF A BUDDHIST MONK
Ajahn Sumedho
Foreword by Jack Kornfield
An instructive and, at times, humorous book drawn from a collection of talks by the abbot of Amaravati Buddhist Centre.
0-946672-23-7

THE ZEN TEACHING OF INSTANTANEOUS AWAKENING
Hui Hai
Trans. John Blofeld
An eighth-century T'ang Dynasty Zen Text.
0-946672-03-2

FINGERS AND MOONS
Trevor Leggett
A collection of humorous and instructive Zen stories and incidents.
0-946672-07-5

ZEN GRAFFITI
Azuki
A book of aphorisms and robust line drawings which point to the practice and fruits of Buddhism. They can nudge us out of apathy, dullness and habit into a direct awareness of the moment's reality. Each reader will respond to different sayings according to individual need and development.
0-946672-24-5

BUDDHISM NOW
A Buddhist journal — interviews, practical advice on living a Buddhist way of life, translations, stories, verse, letters, news, book reviews etc. Six issues a year. (Send £1 or $2 for a sample issue.)